IN A SHEEP'S EYE,
DARLING

In a Sheep's Eye,
DARLING

Margaret Hasse

MILKWEED EDITIONS

IN A SHEEP'S EYE, DARLING
Poems by Margaret Hasse
© 1988 by Margaret Hasse
Printed in the United States of America

91 90 89 88   4 3 2 1

Published by *Milkweed Editions*
Post Office Box 3226
Minneapolis, Minnesota 55403
Books may be ordered from the address above

Designed and Illustrated by R.W. Scholes, © 1988

Library of Congress Catalog Card Number: 87-63532
ISBN 0-915943-25-5

Publication of this book is supported in part by grants from The Dayton Hudson Foundation for Dayton's and Target Stores, The First Bank System Foundation, the Jerome Foundation, the Metropolitan Regional Arts Council from funds appropriated by the Minnesota State Legislature, with special assistance from the McKnight Foundation, the Arts Development Fund of United Arts, and by contributions from many generous individuals, corporations, and foundations.

Poems in this book were written with funds and support from a Loft-McKnight award, a Minnesota State Arts Board grant through an appropriation of the Minnesota State Legislature, and the Ragdale Foundation, Lake Forest, Illinois.

Several of these poems have appeared in *Great River Review*, *Minnesota Monthly*, *Northern Lit Quarterly*, and *WARM Journal*. The author wishes to thank the editors for their permission to include the work here.

The author also wishes to thank the people who improved these poems by suggesting revisions and corrections: Emilie Buchwald, editor of Milkweed Editions; Don Brunnquell, Deborah Keenan, Margot Kriel Galt, members of a writing group; and Wyn Tvedt and Alan Huisman, sensitive readers who are also sensible about grammar and spelling.

To Cindy, Mary Sue,
and other friends, near and far

IN A SHEEP'S EYE, DARLING

I. WOMEN TELLING

II. ONE WOMAN TELLING

I
Women Telling

"My parents, my husband, my brother, my sister."
I am listening in a cafeteria at breakfast.
The women's voices rustle, fulfill themselves
In a ritual no doubt necessary.
I glance sidelong at their moving lips
And I delight in being here on earth
For one more moment, with them, here on earth,
To celebrate our tiny, tiny my-ness.

Czeslaw Milosz, *My-ness*

WOMEN TALKING

to Cheryl and Pat

It was the last summer we were all happy:
one married, one with a new car.
There was a new baby and a slim body among us.
Whenever we met, we acted testy,
pulling at the edges of the tablecloth.
We felt we held a long musical note,
drawing out sound like a line of ribbon.
The end would eventually exhaust us.

"It's so temporary," we say, sounding the "do"
while clinking the glasses
of our love affairs together.
Women with their elbows on the table,
akimbo with talk and drink.
"This man," we'd say, and "that man."
The windows are open; cars brush by like brooms.
We feel we're getting somewhere.

Women, my man friend has said, bind
themselves to other people
through mutual revelation.
And men? Through physical acts, he said.

At our core, we're all hesitant,
the hum of machinery made of glass.
About midnight, the women decide preemptively
that men are more fragile.
At some level, men evade us, as if
they're still playing touch football
on October's fields, feint to the left

just when we think we're close.
They think we'll hold words against them.

That's a point well made, Pat says,
her lips pulsing like a blue fish
in the moment when cigarette smoke makes
its soothing, needy route to her lungs.
Men can sit in duck blinds for hours,
mufflers around their mouths
and feel love for each other.
She expels rings in tight batches.
Too many silences.
They rise up, unraveling, all broken out.

POISON IVY

There, and here. Red pocks, full of puss.
A rash along the thigh.
It's nerves, a colleague says,
but you insist on the real thing,
a brush with leaves in the dense wood.
Two women tell you stories, their outdoor
rolls on viperous green with men
who count now only as part of the memory
of the itch. Wink.

You learn ivy from oak from the nurse
who dispenses lotion that soothes
and reminds you of being yourself,
younger, clean, sitting in booths
in cafes wanting boys to notice
but not touch.
Smelling of Noxzema to their Ben-Gay.

These days you reclaim yourself
from men who want to share your bed,
catch nothing, not play for keeps.
The ivy separates you in clear ways.
You're stubbornly fond of your ailment.
You learn the hard way from sexual battles.
Like a badge of bright red, you feel brave
and you feel the sting.

LOOKING AT LOVE-MAKING: 1

Dreams did not make this moaning.
The couple in the next bunk did, two Dutch lovers,
she on her back with her knees drawn to her chest
like a doe star grazing,
and he, in a slippery, watery movement, tunneled
underground. Both swelling the room
with the wary, ragged edge of sobbing
without sorrow, like slowly tearing
old worn velvet.
This was in Greece in a cavernous co-ed hostel.
Through the shuttered windows,
the Plaka was still awake and the smell of lamb
sputtered oily and dark.
Up the hills, the Acropolis in its injured beauty
was locked for the night; the white limbs
that the sun polished held some of that light.
These love bandits made me edgy,
made me safe, their eyes like the dark of the moon
while mine shone in a pearled wonder at
these lying and locked bodies, as if
inside a bruised plum, the pit,
and inside the pit, the sprout of the seed
fingering its way through.

THE ATTRACTION OF OPPOSITES

Honey rolls out of the plastic tub
like a thick yellow tongue.
You always were a messy chef,
leaving trails of raisins
across the clean tile floor.
Blazes of butter mark the places
your hands have been.
You always have loose ends
of sentences hanging from your mouth.
The tails of your shirts wag.

When you discovered that I parse
my carrots like a sentence,
that my onions are cut in precise
rings like Saturn's,
that my socks always have a mate,
that each paperclip knows
its address in the desk drawer,
that I fear chaos as others
fear the dark, you tore a letter in two.
We each kept half.

When we hold each other,
I keep you from flying apart
into ambitious atoms,
into splinters or lost marbles.
I keep you from being a spilled
button bag, broken pottery, a flight
of birds abandoning each other.
You whisper in my ear
that when you love me, the stars
possess bits and pieces of my heart.

CAMPING OUT

An improbable night found us with armfuls
of blankets, making an obvious pilgrimage
out of the dorm and up
the foothills behind campus.

The setting sun gave more rose.
The chaparral burned with it.
Our faces turned red
with no liquor and no food,
missing nothing.
Dusk robbed the bay of colors by degrees.
Finally, no roommates, no inadvertent others.
Just cattle that came close in the night,
moaning.

GIVING A MASSAGE

The shape of your body suggests:

here, the archipelago down your spine,
here, the dolphin dip of your lower back,
here, the firm reefs of your ribs,
here, the coral in your breasts,
here, the small shells on your fingertips,
here, the shoals near your temples,

here, the deep current of your mouth . . .

LOVING AND DROWNING

When I loved you
I'd swim into the deep water with you.
Strong swimmers both, we'd freestyle towards
the heart of the lake, the place where
it turned to blue diamonds.
Merman and maid, we were
endlessly lovely with our silky tails.

When I loved you,
I swam into the water with you.
I could go anywhere, deeper, deeper.
Suddenly I, with a stitch in my side
like the teeth of an eel,
turned to you for help.
Back on the shore, a shadow
a mile away, you were throwing your voice
like a weird ventriloquist
into the water beside me,
your dummy.

I went down twice, love being
a weak preserver.
But live! Live! I made myself
if only to prove you wrong
about my weak heart
and my forgiving nature.

LOOKING AT LOVE-MAKING: 2

Under the high bridge, a small park.
We used a bench for rest and as a podium.
Five years had slipped by us, two cities:
enough distance to build up a fine
accretion of stories on our tongues.
We kept talking of our work and important lovers.
You told of flying to California to camp
for a weekend with an old flame, a woman
you loved with the needled fascination of a rip.
Into the camp gunned a hundred motorcycles
with twice that many Hell's Angels and their molls.
You quarantined yourselves to your tent
and made the most of the noisy night.
As you talked, over your shoulder I could see
a man and his ghostly woman walk through the woods,
choose a bare spot, take out a blanket,
get naked, slowly.
Your voice did not offend them, and she lay down
on her back, and he pushed into her,
in a flamboyant way, drawing himself
far away from her each time so that
he could look up and down her full body.
I caught all the details and things that weren't.
And you, now, turned and stood stock still, staring.
They were only a loud whisper away from us
but we couldn't manage that.
Our old stories faded as we watched this new one.
How when the couple finished, they both washed

in the river, slowly.
How when the couple left, they smiled at us.
How the woods seemed unearthly and sinning
everywhere, happily, even the birds
in their nests disobeying the dark's mandate
for cover, the streams all falling
into the arms of their mates, the moss clinging
to the muscular wood of our bench.
How our platonic relationship
seemed the shame.

THE PROFIT OF YOUR STORY

to Jean

You are running for exercise
in the first blue hint of dawn.
The lake whispers mirror.
A man with black clothes
jumps from the bushes,
wraps his belt around your neck,
beats you, is ugly to you
in all ways.
You want to wash your body away.

You leave yourself an imprint
in grass, float away.
You lose the words to talk of it,
erase it from all happening.
To have a happy beginning,
middle, ending of your life
was intended.
You want to live the blankness
he made of you.
But you are in a different story,
the one where the heroine
makes herself remember.
His image seen in clouds and rats' faces,
in what sniffs and gnaws,
in gum under tabletops, wadded and tight.

You are at our shoulders,
guardian angel with words
and wings to make our flesh rise
for fear, for flight or
some alertness.

Safety is a choice of parking lot,
a small dog with puncturing barks,
light's promise in an empty house.

You went into the evil forest.
You are the princess, your clothes
torn in little pieces like red petals.
Where the thorns hooked you
are guideposts on the dark path.

You speak, finally,
of water so clear no glass
is needed but the prayer of your hands.
And in that cup, your own voice,
wailing, singing.
Release silence, defend us,
tell us the story to wake us.

You are out running.

You leave yourself an imprint.

You are at our shoulders.

You went into the evil forest.

You speak.

DEATH MASKS

The artist, George Segal, extends the permanence
of death masks to the entire body, capturing
the flesh, spiderlike, in a modern mummified way.
The lovers on the bed, in a white distance
from one another, their limbs bandaged and beautiful.
The man's hand an anchor, his arm over her shoulder.
She's a slim moored boat.
His face against the stone pillow, his slack penis.
The time after love called "the little death."
These two are dying. They've been wounded,
left alone many times when they didn't want to be.
Now left alone together in a clanky bed
in a hotel where the elevator slides
up and down all night long like a blues trumpet,
they keep falling.
One wakes with a brief scream.
Thinking she's saved them both,
she reaches out to him, but he doesn't answer.
He's cut loose from what's difficult in his life,
from moods that shake him like a rag in the wind,
from griefs that love him
like malicious daisies with hearts of gold.
When he finished touching her,
he felt spent and perfect.
He fit his own skin.
He burrowed in towards his white hot heart
and her gardenia perfume, to snow, to marble, to sleep.

*(This Segal sculpture is in the permanent
collection of The Walker Art Center.)*

LEARNING TO LOVE BY HAND

The adolescents, all blind,
cling to me as to a raft.
I walk them over to the sculptures,
lift their hands to greet the artist,
his figures, the ones the museum
lets us touch.
They begin with an elbow, a knee,
stroking it as if it will release
something.
When one discovers an arm,
she is so startled, she says "arm" out loud.
Hands begin to move faster,
like ants or crabs, in a frenzy of touch.
Beggars for alms, their fingers
seek everywhere, into the mouths of the men,
along thighs, in the little valleys
between the breasts of the women;
follow the belly down.
Watching makes me shiver
in the warm anteroom, a witness
to the love-making of those
who first learn longing from stone.

THE SEAMSTRESS

You give me your pants to repair.
You, who haven't been my lover for a long time.
I had nothing to do with the pants being torn,
for it was not from feeding you too much
or too little. Not for a project on my roof
you sacrificed the seam. It was not
in the haste of sexual play with me
nor in any way I saw or knew.
What have you been doing these days?
We have so much to talk about:
where these pants went
when I wasn't with them,
whom they met, where they were washed,
what hour of the night they were taken off
and where they were left when you went to bed.

Here is my hand. Here is the other.
I take your pants with your body absent from them
and I still repair the rents.
Here is my head bent over the tear,
and the fingers all together in one organization.
The frenzied end of the thread finally
licked into submission,
my eyes thread the needle first,
then the thumb and index follow suit.

I say nothing while I work. You, too, sit
with mouth pursed as if sewn that way.
My lips are chapped, feel like
the edges of cotton pulled by hand.
I am torn up by happiness at being used.
This is a rip I don't know what to do with.

II
One Woman Telling

Say It with Flowers.

Patrick F. O'Keefe,
Slogan for the Society of American Florists

MAY

I wish things wouldn't open so wide and be famished.
Today I broke a bloodroot.
A line of orange beads formed on the stem.
Earlier, there had been spring blossoms
like soft tissue beneath a fan of leaves.
The bloodroot's broken stem dried quickly
and seemed to heal as if it were a scratch
and had been bandaided.
The incident seemed as common as the beheading
of a dandelion, poor blond dish that grows.

On my knees, I turn over a rock,
touch off an alarm with my weeding claw.
Ants rush about, their tri-part, pubic bodies.
I lower the lid on the flagstone; panic subsides.

Later, the bloodroot lay shriveled as if it'd been burned.
The voice of the plant called out, was spent.
May is the month my parents died.
The month of May is hungry, has small white hands.

You, you take me and my melancholy,
pet me, call me "poor sweet baby"
without pity, without shame.

JUNE

Perennial flowers are love's timepieces,
antique, inaccurate, recurring.
This is feverfew which looks like a fern
but likes sunshine.
This is the edible orange daylily and this
the "Naked Lady" who returns each fall, surprising us
with her tropical airs.
These are dahlia's Greek complexities.
These, digitalis, like a pole of open-mouthed fish.
And these tender blue departures are forget-me-nots.

Lying beside you some nights I feel like a flower.
Pressed into speech, I'd never name a rose.
Not that extravagant hothouse coil.
Not a violet with its mousey face.
I'd call myself an iris.
I'm fond of her sensual, proud stance.
And you? You're a morning glory
that won't be vased.

We curtail the "I-do," live together
with no vows for a crowd,
only a past rolling beneath us.

JULY

We're driving off the heat.
Ten-thirty at night and still eighty degrees.
The warm air is a hand laid on me.
The dipper's pouring out its water of darkness.
"Driving through the night, going fast . . . "
The father in that novel left his family
to drive and drive . . .

You like to drive. By yourself.
In your old Volvo, just a bone itself.
You can stick your feet through,
touch pavement, touch stone.

My father used a car for his private departures.
At Christmas, on long weekends.
Other times when the family's weight fell
like an endless boom,
a great thud of joyless obligation.
Our men, deprived of the right to fuss with intimacy,
to groom the details of relationship,
to be tiny and trivial and set,
rush away from the women,
choosing from among many kinds of silence
other lovers, night, violence, work.

Tonight I'm in the dark car
inside a silence we share.
We drive down Lake Street, by thousands of neon lights:
car lots, restaurants, billboards.

Talking won't save us.
Not the moon in its perfect banana boat.
Not the art you make with its solid Russian look.
Not my begonia dressed in magenta and green.
Not my money or your need to keep it simple.
In an endless list of useless aids,
I locate a once and future thing, desire.
I touch you, want you to touch me.
Stars are burning bodies, and I am one.

AUGUST

Summer is going, a lover slipped from the bed.
Last night I bought the weekend groceries near midnight.
The slim boy who carried them to the car
worked and hefted like a man,
said it was a fantastic night,
so softly warm,
said he didn't like fall,
said there's no mercy in winter.

Looking at his face, fresh as lettuce, and lacy,
I wondered what was recalled in the lessening of the sun,
what he knew beyond the cosmetic tan of the other boys
that made him mention mercy.

Across the long black lakes,
in the yards, crickets pant,
little rough lungs.
A few cars cross paths on the hot roadmap of the city.
Too late for movies, too late for bars.
People, like me, gone out for something:
cat food, milk and eggs, the paper,
contact with a stranger, this boy
who provokes a flamboyant tenderness.
In the garden, the last chrysanthemums
toss their lavender pompoms into the air.

SEPTEMBER

Once out too deep and alone in a lake,
I felt a premonition
of muscle cramps and the water shuddered
as if a bird high overhead blotted out my entire sun.
Believe me, we can be more afraid in one moment
than a whole lifetime of thought thinks possible.

When you disappeared under your car at work
by the garage light on an internal obstinacy
of metal, a duplicate of myself
thought I'd never see you again.
The veranda was smattered with wet yellow leaves.
Slugs, they stick to the house, the roof, my skin,
cause a leopard pattern of yellow against
summer's tan turned pale.

Dusk has backed up to my work schedule.
A new dread walking from the bus.
In yards, the garden hoses snake among petunias
which give off an awful, final smell.
No frost yet, but each night holds glittery potential.
I've dug up the tender bulbs,
dahlias are packed like glass in sawdust,
gladiolas in brown grocery bags.

Had I spoken out loud, I'd have said to you:
"I just wanted to see if you're really there."

In bed you lie
heavy and dark as a lake.
I touch you lightly,
here, there, trolling for your body.
You aren't available.
I cannot swim in you, can only
lift my hands, water falling through
the fingers as fish through a broken net.

OCTOBER

The road stoops to darkness,
the fringed shawl of ravines drawn in.
Lights of distant houses jet
like blue pilots in ovens.
Plumes of white from the chimneys
jiggle the backdrop of bare trees.
Inside their brick house, our friends
with the Biblical names—Ruth and Joseph—
work, oblivious to our car's crunch
on snow in the long driveway.
Inside the hull of the car, we sit
to appreciate their stronghold,
our grip on each other's hand diminishing.

They're in the kitchen together.
Joseph on the counter dangling his feet
like fish lines.
Ruth prepares the dinner,
cracking the heads of lettuce
in her capable hands.
The door flashes open.
We're gulped in and darkness left
to hang around the edges of the yard,
a prowling animal among hooded pine.

Joseph has the dark curly hair
of another country where the holy map
is shredded in fists.

When he found his home in the country,
he drew a circumference
around nine acres and settled in.

Ruth will not keep a Christmas tree
out of respect for his religion.
Her faith will open, take in his.
Precise instructions aren't necessary
for her survival.
She waves the brown hair of cross-breeding,
the insouciant flag of America.

Ruth's father tells Joseph
he hasn't seen his daughter so happy
since she was sixteen.
"What have you been feeding her?" he asks.
Ruth, the daughter of Wendell.
Ruth, the daughter of Brooke.
Wendell and Brooke, son and daughter
of couples extending over the hill of time.

NOVEMBER

A business coming back into vogue:
matchmaking.
The one key to success is whether both people
say "yes" to the image
of two of a kind
who pass out of their vows
to the white orchid of death.
Wanting is the important thing,
not the perfect fit.

Once a question about the future has formed,
it has to emerge, like a slippery thing in an egg,
slithery, wanting.
You remind me of my father,
his chin set in an empire of no.

Who'd want to bed with a turtle
except the other turtle left in the world,
overjoyed by the sight of a shell?
Who'd want to sleep with a swan
except when times are tough
and fairy tales invented?
Who'd want a wolf except to start Rome?
Who'd want you, except me who has come to want?
Who has come to faith
that mating makes sense?
Me, I have. Not you.

DECEMBER

We begin to barter. I'll give you
this poem, privacy, if
you'll give me a child.
You give me cleaning and I'll give you a home.
You let me talk and I'll let you alone.

We get angry, mouths like slashes
cut meals into little pieces.
The poinsettia's leaves are serrated knives.
We fight over a phrase in French.
Neither of us knows French.
We stand in the kitchen, unable to touch
at all the wrong times.
I eat my words, bits of stale bread.
You tighten your hands and loosen them
like squeezing mud into the shapes of sausage.

Packed full as boxes of Kleenex,
we take a hiatus from pain,
hike down towards the ice rink,
a cool metallic sheen
revealed under a light brushing of old snow.
The trees are stripped and gorgeous.
New snow tinkers with the air.
Hoarfrost thickens on every branch,
on the O.K. chain of the backstop
where a ball field begins its buried sleep.
The yard next door is littered with children.
Their kite-like bodies make snow angels.

You pull me into the house
by the cross of bone above my heart.

Larger flakes buzz near the window
like a swarm of white moths.
And we hold each other
for an impossibly long last time,
our fingers blind as snow, falling everywhere
over our separate bodies.

JANUARY

Some people establish their lives
like place settings sold only in pairs.
That easy.
Some do it with joy, their hands
on the spoons in the full drawers,
silver anchoring the room.
Married people have their reasons.

Your large hands grope, drop silverware,
crackling with despair.
You don't want to be fed on any schedule.
You don't want to feed.
You need to leave.
I need to let you leave.
Suddenly you're gone.

One spoon in my hand needs polish.
The tarnish smears off to reveal my face,
upside down, of strange size,
the cheeks ballooning,
the tiny pin head and chin pointed as a goatee.
Dipping my spoon's bowl into a watery soup
I lay down my prayer:
that things are exactly as they must be.

I think of churches.
Of my life closing twice
as Emily said, dear Emily.
Is my god only a god of hard times?
I seek out churches,
pretending to be Catholic.
I want an ancient,
a bloody Christ, a red rose and

a thorn for my vision.
Each paraffined muscle in agony.
Loss is inside everything.
I fall to my knees, and further.

FEBRUARY

Each night there's a new thing in bed with me
and I wrestle for hours.
I want to fall away from bitterness
of the defection.
I want to fall asleep.
There's no failsafe to the parachute
and I keep falling.

I rise in the morning with sorrow
I try to assuage
with bread and milk and coffee.
There is nothing to be done
but eat the sorrow with the bread.

I shake off my husk, wash my face,
turn on the radio, wait for the weather report
which is sure to be bad.
The house lumbers toward dawn with me on its back.

The blast furnaces of the birds die down,
I find their stone carcasses.
No fuel at all in the lumpish snow.
I dress my ice in a suit,
collect myself into my car,
my soft hair bunned, my face made up,
my legs cool and useless in their shrill shoes.
A public self keeps on, keeps going.
So that I have something to do,
I save my grocery lists until Saturday.
I buy myself amaranths with their frozen hearts.
I make long distance phone calls,
let people hug me, tell me again

how much they like me.
I hang on to commitments, feed the birds,
let go of events I didn't like anyway.

I quit saying he was smart at games,
the best at Boggle.
I take down photos of him from the refrigerator,
stack them, face on face on face.
I put his socks in a garbage bag
and move into his bureau drawers.

The lantern of the moon shines.
I turn off all the lights in the house,
stay awake to watch the nothing,
the great whiteness, a whiteness to the bone.
Beyond whiteness, what?
The moon's skeleton, bone again.
What color's marrow?
A bone is Penelope, all her loyal muscles
beside the sea, situated in the posture of waiting.
In a chair, at some useful work
she wants to throw down, but holds on.
I want to be used, used well, made use of.
I want to be useful, be a quilt
over a child's skin.
Useful as a knife through beans' green sickles,
making a meal of rich vegetables.
Useful as a man holding a woman,
giving her what she wants from him.

Under my clothes my small body
is a large surprise of bones and greediness.
Remember, I say to myself, you were often lonely
when he was here.
This loneliness is familiar.
I finger myself like prayer beads,
without belief.

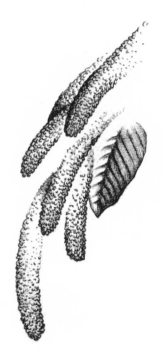

MARCH

Made humble with loss, I work
at the little low projects around the house
with a new love for them.
I wake up, work, watch the degrees
of mercury huddle above freezing.
Keeping busy becomes the acolyte of bravery.
Outside, I think of the hundred
red mouths of the tulips, telling secrets,
underground.
I climb the silver rungs of a ladder
to the top of my house, pull
the sodden slag of leaves from the gutters,
pick at dams of ice.
No one's down there to hold the ladder steady.
I look down in the role of angel
to the white pillows of snow.
I'd never pitch myself down;
too much curiosity makes me careful.
Everything that happens to me
succeeds in passing away
in an interesting manner.

APRIL

How the sky is filleted with pink.
How the oak tree keeps some of her leaves to herself
deep into winter and the next spring.
How the pines keep all their leaves,
dark hugging shapes in the dawn.
How now the pink is fled from the sky.
How I wander with my eyes into the garden,
brown, absent of blossom, a pursed withholding,
a watchful presence.
Finally, the first bird at the feeder,
a normal sparrow, his tintype heart.
Now the carlights on the freeway are being turned off.
Now I see two raccoons by the bushes.
How animals seem to find each other easily.
How the animals lumber into the ark.
The tom cat and his diminutive wife.
The slow slosh of lions, their tails,
two tan rumps with great cushions of fur.
The solicitous woodpecker
and her proud, uniformed mate.
The grey clouds of elephants.
The armored cockroaches.
Two frogs in their green hurrahs.
Two tenderhearted doves.
Ruth and Joseph,
Wendell and Brooke,
Paulette and Jeff,
Jay and Kathy,
each kind, carrying their accouterments
to consecrate their longing.
And something extra humans have:

the language of promise.
These two ways of crawling inside a place
at once so foreign and familiar,
our true singleness
stands briefly in abeyance.

MAY

A squirrel dallies on a limb, making it sway
as a child might, riding the branch to a gallop.
The backyard's leathery and patchy white.
I want to own all the corners of my house,
bake bread from honey and winter's wheat.
Goodbye to the cold.
Welcome, spring, you wild blue kite.
Tomorrow the thermometer will break sixty.
The flowers catch the fever,
rush toward their season.
The lilacs, shy guests;
violets the size of blue-tip kitchen matches.
After its solid state, the earth
begins stretching for a new map.
The yard, a slick wet black.
The garden, where I dig, a wet and deeper black.
Under the patched and dented snow,
the green begins its old new song.
Tridents prick the dirt: day lilies.
Standing by the back window, I'm happy.
I think about it a while.
It's still true.

III
Postcards Stacked To Be Mailed

"This they tell, and whether it happened so or not
I do not know; but if you think about it,
you can see that it is true."

Black Elk quoted in *Black Elk Speaks*
John G. Neihardt

OCTAGONAL MILLS AT DAWN

Kinderdijk-complex, The Netherlands

Dearest Marg,

Living here so long
I hardly see the beauty;
it takes a postcard
to explain everything
again to me.
Look, see—
the way the colors spill
over the edges of the mills,
their sulking dark.
Then rose, rose.
When I was a child, no one
wanted to teach art.
It opened the hearts
too wide.
One polite project was allowed me:
I opened the crayola box
to the crayons
like a choir on risers,
then lavished white paper
with color, mashing the crayons
down to their paper wraps.
Then inked the entire sheet,
a black plague.
With the points of scissors,
I brought back select colors
like the hand of god.
The pictures were of daybreak
always. Forever
I'll see the world at that hour

with those eyes, a new power.
I hope that you're doing better these days,
that the pain has broken.

  I love you, Mary Sue

GREETINGS FROM FLORIDA,
THE SUNSHINE STATE

Tampa, Florida

Hey Margo,

This is the view from my window,
the orange groves, the butterfly
with its proboscis deep into blossoms.
Everything rhymes, the orange
of the fruit, the delicate insides
of the waxy flowers,
the color plates inside the black-lined
windows of the monarch's wings.
You told me of your first time
in Florida, taking the car
off the interstate,
to side roads, parking in a grove.
You got high from the smell,
punch-drunk on orange blossom,
thousands of acres of trees,
each one wearing a little scarf
of sweetness.
My father died last week
taking with him the odor of hospital,
acrid medicine and feces.
Although the windows were open
and the trees in bloom,
rot tunneled underneath all other smell,
cracked open the surface, split rinds.
I must leave Florida soon, before
the orange rotates on its slim green stem,
falls, puss yellow.

John

BLACK CAT
Minneapolis, Minnesota

Eric—

Cat king of the yard
presides over a throne of warmth,
a sidewalk in the sun.
Nearby, the shady garden, vegetables
with their fawning leaves.
Although it was hot and still today
the cat asserted his rights over
the failed pilgrims of flight.

I saw the king squeeze himself, leap.
Lost bird was dandled,
released, gathered in again
to be raked on his side with nails.
The cat killed what lived in the throat
of the robin, and dragged to my door
the heart in its damaged package.
The cat now wears
a ruby around his neck,
an amulet of blood in his white ruff.

Margaret

VISIT TO A CEMETERY WITH FACES

Florence, Italy

Dear sister,

These tombstones wear faces
on their faces, small
photos encased in plastic,
little friends left behind
by the ones who stepped back
and out of the gates.
I would not have left her,
our little mother,
not an angel for the snow,
not a public album
for strangers to see
like the movie marquee
with a naked girl
we knew from high school.
We must face up, she is gone.
The mother is gone away
with her warm arms.
We buried ashes,
resembling, as you said,
a handful of soft shells.

Trudy

GOOD SHOPPING AND DELICIOUS FOOD

Lucerne, Switzerland

Marg,

And how is Europe for me?
I'm making my way through
cheese and chocolate,
baked goods and French sauces.
Bratwursts on the street
in Stuttgart, Belgian waffles,
rijsttafel in Amsterdam,
and, by the Mediterranean,
Italian ice and gyros.
Nothing to drink for me, thanks.
I'll pass on ouzo to honor baklava.
Europe on Five Pounds a Week:
I wrote the book, was paid
twenty pounds total gain.
I'm packed tight
as my valise, over-stuffed
with leather straps straining.
In October I'll come
rolling, rolling home.
Pork pie, potato girl.
I can order dessert
in eight languages.

Nancy

ARTICHOKE FIELDS

San Jose, California

Dear Margie,

We're arrived; we have an apartment.
We've unpacked our pots and pans,
made our first meal. Beginners,
we boiled the artichoke an hour.
Its green descended to moss and brown.
It wore its ancient armor
like a militant turtle.
We peeled off the pointed leaves
and ate dabs of meat
with lemon and butter
hoping something would happen.
To find the slippery heart
was to be children again
getting more than we deserved.

Gordi and Janet

SUMMERTIME IN THE CITY

New York, New York

Friend,

The apartment is so close
we cannot bear it, think
of you on your deck.
Outside two moons glow.
One, a streetlight;
the other, authentic,
luminous in the smog,
is in full bloom.
It shines fierce
on the shy ears
of jack rabbits,
silver on wolves' hair.
Slips of the moon
get in our eyes,
take root during the night.
Our pupils become plots
of wild light
which can be harvested
on a hot city day
when we know
we weren't made
to live like this.

Bernie and Alan

CHRISTO: RUNNING FENCE
Sonoma and Marin Counties, California

Mik'l!

Hearings were held, you know.
Folks scratched their heads, said
why spend money to set up a white fence
for no particular reason,
just to take it down again.
It's a fair question.
The fence of silk ran all the way
to the ocean, then submerged
like a glad gift to the sea.
The orange light through the curtains
at dusk, the white sheets,
a laughter in the wind.
I think of dancers who put their best
foot forward, offer themselves to air.
As close a cousin to a kite as I've seen.
Come out to see it, run alongside it
like a perplexed horse,
full of green grass and gallop.

xoM

GOLDEN FLEECE IN MAMMOTH CAVE

Mammoth Cave National Park, Kentucky

Hi.

The onyx flowstone on this card
is like the overflow of a giant waxy candle
that lighted our nights.
Although we're of different generations,
I too listened to Joni Mitchell,
lit candles in the Sixties to talk
all night about the war, how men
performed suspicious acts in offices.
Fathers fumbled with us, patting
our heads, treating our ears
like handles of coffee cups.
Now a father myself, I recognize
their humble manners of affection.
They didn't know how to be like
mothers, with their sweet pies,
bedside talks and tuck-ins,
their warm clasps, their chatter.
Our fathers had lost a foothold
in the earth, wore their suits gingerly.
We thought them capable of great wrongs.
We were proud of our shiny new conversations
and our ability to travel about the world.
Standing by me, once, our last time, at a lake,
you said the racing swimmers resembled
wounded birds, the wild splashing.
I envied you your precision to describe.
I never told my father I loved him.

Les

FISHERMEN MAKE THEIR LIVING

Skyros, Greece

Dear Rex,

A fisherman pulls his salmon-colored nets
from the blue Aegean. Bent over on the beach,
I catch an angle of the island out of the corner
of my eye. I stop, sit for an hour,
watch the light change to darkness,
lose the laborer to the lullaby sea
or to his house and wife where lamb is eaten
with lots of garlic. I'm homesick.
Above me in the sky, a chunk of grey stone
seems to rise. Rises, higher than the horizon.
On its cool white surface a man has walked.
Did he dream of planting the familiar marigolds
and petunias, a row of midwestern windbreaks,
a hedge of extravagant lilac?

Margie

BITTERROOT, STATE FLOWER

Chinook, Montana

Dear Aunt Margie,

The two blooms look exploded.
The magenta for Montana backed
by a dry twiggy setting,
the insides, delicate, fuzzy.
I'm at home here, finally,
though I'm not courageous
as you say–for moving so often:
ten addresses in five years.
The bitterroot does have
an amazing center,
the perfection of purple.
I feel at the fulcrum
of teetering and tottering.
When I rise in the morning, happy,
I wonder: will I pay dues for this?
When I see green, I see ghosts.
Do I talk too much,
ambitious and hot?
I'm a mouth hungry for sunshine:
these flowers, casting beauty.
Beauty, yes, enthusiasm,
close to god, but exploding,
exploding, flying apart.

Ann

BEAUTIFUL TROPICAL BIRDS

Captiva Island, Florida

Dear Margie,

This is an accurate picture of Florida
as I know it. Just subtract
the blue sky and beautiful tropical birds.
What's left is fog and gulls.
Walks at dawn suit me.
I like my coffee dark and sad.
The shoreline is an arm
bent around the water.
When I was little and at the movies,
my father would stretch
his cramped arm, leave it
on the back of my seat.
I'd sit up straighter,
feel his skin molecules from mine,
pretend he was hugging me,
warm as the caterpillar velvet
of the old upholstery.
I remember the first movie I remember:
"To Kill a Mockingbird."
We all wanted a father like Atticus,
a strong man at the center of things.
The second movie was "A Night to Remember"
where the shame was men dressed as women
claiming spaces in lifeboats,
jewelry strapped to their ankles.
Those movies made impressions.
I vowed to tell the truth,
hate money, never ride in ships.

Jim

PERFECT HOUSE
IN THE PRAIRIE ARCHITECTURE STYLE
Red Wing, Minnesota

Dear Annie,

Occasionally you become acquainted
with a house so perfect
you'd stay forever if you could.
Someone already lives here.
I saw a woman peeking from the back garden,
wearing a small star hat
and looking shy as a Korean girl.
I turned away. Such regret:
I have only one body to live in.
I sit across the street.
The building is a giant calligraphed letter.
It reveals itself slowly
like a face we've decided to love.
The windows open out. How I'd like to push
the little cranks in their small orbits
every day, opening the windows
for the evening, the tatters of cool air.
Then close them slightly against the heat
of July mornings, living in a kimono
in that burnt sienna and wood house
on orange juice and apples, being happy
in a way we're never really happy
except for a moment, except for now.

Best, Margie

IV
Stunned By The Eye

"The great revelation had never come. The great revelation perhaps never did come. Instead there were little daily miracles, illuminations, matches struck unexpectedly in the dark . . . "

Virginia Woolf, *To the Lighthouse*

STARTING WITH THE VINE

How I love the vine that grows beneath the north window,
a vine without much to say for itself,
just a few odd phrases of berries and leaves,
just that.
How I love the glitter on the cabbage,
something like a sliver, something like in a silver ring,
something like that.
How I love the way light hangs in the air of the room,
stillness falling in a particulate way,
the curtains, quiet and aired, the oncoming of fall.
How I love the photographs of friends,
my sister with her glossy smile,
the boys with their liver-soft baseball mitts,
the children of gypsies who live in the South.
How I love how foreign my house feels
when the self subtracts its overbearing interests
except for love, love falling like light,
vacant and illuminating.

HIRED GARDENER

He came at a price leaving
a note when he left:
"Lost on what are flowers
and what are weeds."
He hoped his work met my approval
and billed me.
I held the paper
and looked at pillage.
The would-be gardener
had uprooted the forget-me-nots,
pummeled the petunias,
unveiled the bridal veil
before her time.
He'd unwrapped the soft soil
from the trillium roots,
disregarded the infancy
of the pansies, twisted noses
from the nasturtiums.
Much in little, Thoreau said,
in Latin, and Pete, the gardener,
evidently understood.
I had been given too many
irises to be pure.
I'd lived beyond my day lily means.
I had to give up tulips, daffodils
in order to rise
to a spiritual plane, look down
on the clarified earth,
the grave of these blossoms,
the celebrations of the soil,
bright, lost pleasures.

LOVING WHAT IS NOT ALWAYS GOOD

Today, the steady drop of Minnesota rain.
It's the same rain everywhere.
It's water and we need it.
The oak leaves are like claws.
Let me stand in this cold rain
and not abandon you.
A million pin pricks of the rain.
Like the lights, you are lit.
Like the home, you are not forgotten.

This losing you is hard,
your tall laughter, your free dance.
You beat yourself up with drink
and dark nights and too many men
who cared for you temporarily.
You used them, and they used you,
riding to a sweat with a furor.
Crying alarms on top of each other.

Once, in a cheap hotel in Quebec,
I woke to hear screaming through the walls,
murderous shrieks which were desire.
How we embrace our tyrants.
How we love our own foot
though a toenail is in-grown
and we limp in tight shoes.
We love the pit of our stomach
where the pain resides.

THE MEMORIAL WAY: VIET NAM

And here, the guide says, the memorial
to the war some of you can remember.

The memorial's a study in two decades
which slant towards us, and away
like a giant hinge.
We keep looking over our shoulders
as if our spines were spiral.
What do we see?
A door in the ground only
Orpheus can budge.

Above, a brief cliff
overhung with Whitman's curls,
the grass.
We are the living and the were-living.
We, the dead and the yet-to-be-dead.

If we lay our faces to this hard water,
it's cool like the day-old dead.
Stepping back, we're mirrored.
The men mark us from their niche.
A long mantra of names, the chant
in stone, row on row,
neat etchings, year by year
chiseled in the fine, shiny black.

We are shades beside the tomb
on our little path, with flowers.

THE HOUSE MAY BE BURNING

But keep writing.
Write by the glow of the windows,
the roof alight
like a red-haired girl,
you in the back yard, safe.

The ladybug's flown away.
Recall her flit and armored crawl.
To the last breath of summer.
Upon the circular of winter.

The man may have left.
This doesn't stop
the writing. Between
the pages, a slight blur.
The man may have been old
and ill, or young
who stopped trying
to be with you.
Ghost days.

You're swimming across
a deep lake with a soul
you're making.
You save the swimmer,
the sailor,
the drowned,
the damned
and the beloved.

GIRL IN THE GRASS

The splatter of heat on the open lawn.
The drowsy, distant motors.
A tickle of ants, their shortcut across your leg.
Perhaps you're nine, a penny for each dandelion,
if you include its hairy root. If there are spiders,
they don't hurt. If there are boys, and mean,
it goes to show they like you.
If you are lonely, build a nest from grass clippings
and populate it with flying horses, and eggs.
If you want to, lie back.
The wind herds its animal cracker clouds
across the sky.
If you are tired, crawl on your hands and knees
into the shade.
Not all the shiny dandelions dead
could buy you this sleep again.

MOVIES AND GREY LIGHT

Take one boy. Take one boy out of the house.
On his own. One five-year-old boy. At night.
Take one long field beyond the drive-in movies.
This is West Virginia where I'm taking you.
Back to a young boy's reason for running off.

Back to his family's house. His mother adores
rummage sales: salt and pepper shakers,
piggybanks and doilies, little thimbles,
walls wallpapered with patterns and
pictures on top of floral designs.
He wants to look at everything
as if with a peacock's thousand eyes.
Sight is an enormous burden.
For a boy whose eyes are wide-open and wild,
a place with much in it can be a kaleidoscope,
all dizziness and disorder.
Even though the house is remarkably busy,
his mother doesn't say, "Don't touch."
But why touch what pains you?

The black night is not cluttered
with anything but stars.
He squeezes out the back door like toothpaste.
The outdoor movies attract him,
one beam of light from the genie
projecting from booth to screen.
The faces are big and absorbing.
Big trees and horses and big kisses.
Only one place to look.
Sometimes the police find him in the open fields

beyond the hunched cars.
He thinks they are nice, carrying him home,
half-asleep in their trunky arms.

Thirty years later. Take this boy to be a man.
Alone in an apartment in the Midwest.
His possessions minimum in number,
sequestered in closets.
He barely wants his furniture.
Nothing on the walls. From the windows,
the scene is a high, urban simplicity.
The colors are chrome and grey.
There is a TV by the bed. He loves movies,
falls asleep by their flickering light.

OPEN TO NEW THINGS

When you leave me today, you are smiling and your
hair is wet. Later I chide you for the hair. Yes,
mama, you say, and I say I'm not. Not your mama, your
wife. I'm not your divorced past or a student from
your school. I'm somebody new who didn't know what
you're teaching, that the opening "C" in Celtic is
hard, that to keep from freezing your skin on the
lake, you keep brushing off frost that keeps trying
to form tiny cobwebs on your cheek. I didn't know
the first thing about music, except you said the first
thing is that you admit you like it and are willing
to learn and listen and learn. Listen! That's the
main thing. Sitting still in a room with music and
listening hard, each phrase smashing something in
your heart in a delicate way.

MOTHER, WATCHING HER DAUGHTER SLEEP

Her polite body smells of milk and a faint salt.
She curls on her side in bed.
She is sailing. The shores are strewn
with bright ribbons.

The curve of her clear-skinned nostrils
are shells. She holds her hands closed
as if they are full of secrets.
I stand still as if near a great body of water.

It's hard to imagine my sleep was ever
that easy; my breathing smooth and moist
as a humidifier. My body that small and unused.
I am near magic to have made her.

AT THE FIRST FALSE SIGN OF MY WOMANHOOD

The first time was a mistake in identity,
three drops as from a needle's bite.
The blood coagulated into hard rubies
the toilet swallowed.
Mother gave me a box of immense pads
and a book. *Being Thirteen*
I read with a creepy, suspended feeling
as if I were being held up in front of my family
as a naked baby with breasts.
Then I grew big suddenly, was dumped
into the bin of womanhood.

That night, a pillow over my head
to stifle my ragged breathing, I tried
to think of myself as the book described,
an emerging flower, a woman promised.
My temperature climbed
into the high brain of hallucination.
A spider at the window, hairy and friendless.
A clock tromping to get me.
The centers of my hands thinned.

As it turned out, this experience was not to be
period, it was virus. I'd been taken in.
It was the right time for fertility, not disease.
And my mother had been eager to get me across
the border, thinking that I would not hear

her trembling whisper, the one from a woman
with a mastectomy, a husband who hid,
and flesh falling to its knees with age.
The body betrays you was the message
this fifty-five-year-old mother didn't want
her child to hear, but out it came
over the hand across the mouth
of someone screaming.

GOING ON ALONE IN THE GREAT CONVERSATION

Mother, you used to say that old was
just going on, no special feeling,
except of surprise.
You said that dead was a great conversation
continued. With the stars? I wondered.
With the living? With dreamers taken up
in sex or death?

Mother, the last time I saw you was last night
though you have been dead ten years.
Like fire in a paper, your face flamed,
each line and hair, both lips and hands
coveted in their sweet perfection.
Your only fault: you didn't stay
long enough. I want to talk with you.
With luck, your hands would pet my hair
which can never be touched enough.
With time, I could have smelled your smell,
yellow perfume, the dry flower of makeup.
Instead, after a glimpse of you, I was like
a child on the green grass
in the sputter of tulips, the parent departing
in the big black car.
I cry after it: "Come back.
Take me with you. Me go along."

Me go on alone. Much later when
I am seventy, your age when you died,
old mother, I'll be your twin widow in the mirror.
We will both be wearing lavender,
absurd Easter hats and smiles because

we've faith in what's new and what is given.
Because we loved reading out loud,
the words, each one a new penny dropped in a jar.
Because we loved walking.
Because we have kneeled at each other's sick beds,
and you passed on the little secret notes
and the gene codes, these bow legs from you,
these valentine eyes, this sentimental breathing.
Because we are each a word
in a great conversation, and the word is good.

IN A SHEEP'S EYE, DARLING

to Yofe, to Richard, to marriage

All day in biology class you'd been looking hard
at everything put in front of you on the counter
as if you were starving for these sights:
a tree frog's beating heart, lichen from a tree,
swamp water's industrious community.
Even wax from your ear under a magnifying glass
made you bend lower, awed at the gunk
your body produces.
If this is what we slough off, how amazing
attached cells must be, you thought, and carefully
scraped some from the inside of your cheek.
The cells were blurred, like a smudged charcoal
drawing, just the way you imagined cheek cells
to be, not the precision of liver, not brain.
You knew you didn't know much about this,
and were probably wrong, but you loved
your own excitement, as if you were the first
person to open another in an operation
and discover all the organs under
a slipcover of fascia like tender offspring.

All this looking set you up to be stunned by the eye.
And you stared back at the big dismembered thing,
the way it sat in its socket like a pearl
in a soft oyster, like an oiled, see-through marble.
The cornea, tiny and perfect in its convexity,
and the lens, the way it flattened and thickened

in the center, white irregular filaments running
through it, as if some sight shattered inside
or some sight held, all sewn up.

The teacher thought it unlikely your wife
would share your thrill, but let you
carry the eye home in your backpack,
in the baggie left over from lunch, and you two
bent over it in the bright fluorescence of kitchen
and noticed the irrigation system of blood vessels,
and the soggy iris, and the cornea
and talked about what you could see being
only the tiniest part of the eye, and the eye
only a small part of the sheep, and the sheep
a small part of the farm and the earth and the universe,
and you went to bed too awed to have sex.
That night you dreamed of the great grass
of sheep fields, the way it looked to the sheep
who stuck her head into it seeking
a particular blade, and the color green
welled up inside you like tears, and you woke.

Margaret Hasse's first collection of poems was *Stars Above, Stars Below* (New Rivers Press, 1984). She has taught writing in the Poets-in-the-Schools programs of several states, in community colleges, and in prisons. She holds a B.A. in English from Stanford University and an M.A. from the University of Minnesota. Her honors include a Minnesota State Arts Board grant and a Loft-McKnight award in poetry. She lives in Minneapolis, Minnesota, with her husband, and works as executive director of the Minnesota Alliance for Arts in Education.